HAUS CURIOSITIES

The Responsibilities of Democracy

About the Contributors

Claire Foster-Gilbert is the founder director of the Westminster Abbey Institute. A public philosopher and author, Foster-Gilbert has played an instrumental role in the medical research ethics field and has led efforts to shift the Church's thinking on environmental issues.

The Rt Hon Sir John Major KG CH was Prime Minister of the United Kingdom and Leader of the Conservative Party from 1990 to 1997.

The Rt Hon Sir Nicholas Clegg was Leader of the Liberal Democrats for eight years from 2007 and Deputy Prime Minister from 2010 to 2015. He is currently Vice-President for Global Affairs and Communications at Facebook.

Edited and with an Introduction by Claire Foster-Gilbert

THE RESPONSIBILITIES OF DEMOCRACY

John Major and Nick Clegg

First published by Haus Publishing in 2019
4 Cinnamon Row
London SW11 3TW
www.hauspublishing.com

The right of the authors to be identified as the authors
of this work has been asserted in accordance with
the Copyright, Designs and Patents Act 1988

A CIP catalogue record for this book is
available from the British Library

Print ISBN: 978-1-912208-73-9
Ebook ISBN: 978-1-912208-74-6

Typeset in Garamond by MacGuru Ltd

Printed in Czech Republic

Contents

Acknowledgements

Sincere thanks are due to the Dean and Chapter of Westminster, the Council of Reference, Fellows and Steering Group of Westminster Abbey Institute, Andrew Blick, Ruth Cairns, Mark Easton, Raa Gillon, Charles Haddon-Cave, Harry Hall, Alice Horne, Kathleen James, Igor Judge, Richard Luce, Seán Moore, Clare Moriarty, Jean-Francois Oliva, Barbara Schwepcke, Gillian Stamp and Simon Surtees.

Introduction

Claire Foster-Gilbert

The role of Westminster Abbey Institute is to nurture and revitalise moral and spiritual values in public life. It does not comment on policy nor campaign for any particular cause. It seeks to offer only those contributions to an active, noisy debate about politics and government that reach to the deep moral and spiritual roots of these institutions in a way that is timely, but also timeless. The essays by Sir John Major and Sir Nicholas Clegg in this book, first given as lectures in Westminster Abbey in 2017, have these qualities. They are only lightly edited because their observations about what threatens and what encourages a healthy democracy were salient at the time they were delivered and remain salient now.

It would be otiose, in a 2019 publication, to ignore the context of the Brexit challenge that is dominating British political and social life. Both Major and Clegg refer extensively to it. The challenge has not diminished in the two years since they spoke – on the contrary – and so this introduction will analyse further the implications for democracy of the Brexit years. It will do so in the spirit of the Institute's role: not by taking sides, but by highlighting the underlying moral and spiritual stresses the Brexit years have brought upon our public service institutions and the people who work in them, looking in turn at Parliament and government; the Civil Service; and the Judiciary. It will make a plea for a greater understanding and cherishing of our long-established constitutional settlement, as well as for its continuing moral evolution, not its thoughtless destruction.

Parliament and government

The unwritten British constitution puts parliamentary sovereignty at its heart. Parliament is the supreme legal authority in the UK and it can create or end any law.[1] Though they will take its views into account, elected members of the House of Commons can override members of the House of Lords and so, in practice, it is our elected representatives who have the final responsibility to determine the law. This system makes democratic government pre-eminent, which means, rightly, that the people – the *demos* – determine who will govern their country.

Seeking election by the people means politicians need to feed and respond to the wishes and wants of the people, make themselves popular and, usually, show charisma. These qualities can sometimes make for unstable and unprincipled leadership. Politicians almost always seek office in order to improve the lives of others, but they want to be recognised for it too. They are willing to play for high stakes and risk sudden tumbles from grace, and they can have fragile egos behind their apparently tough public carapaces. If a politician is virtuous and wise, we are lucky: these qualities are not listed in a politician's job description, and nor does the electorate tend to look for them. An astonishing and telling poll conducted by *The Sunday Times* during the July 2019 Conservative leadership contest showed that well over 50% of us would not buy a secondhand car from one of the contenders, but well over 50% of us would like him to be prime minister.[2] As Jonathan Sumption pointed out in his 2019 Reith Lectures, the 2015 election demonstrated that the electorate does not reward compromise, arguably one of the most important qualities in politics and certainly much needed now. We resoundingly did not vote for the Liberal Democrats who had compromised their policies in order to make the coalition Government of 2010–2015 work.[3] Sumption calls elections 'auctions of promises', and Clegg in his essay concurs. Politicians who stand on doorsteps at election time confessing that they won't be able to achieve much during their time in office because external events tend to dominate and influence most government agendas but that they will do their best under the circumstances, will not gain votes, however honest the confession. Election promises must be strong, substantial and certain, despite the reality that ensues once a party is in power.

These are the fallible people who become our elected representatives in our sovereign Parliament. Their responsibility is pre-eminent, and they are subject only to conventions that have evolved over hundreds of years, to which Chris Bryant's magisterial history of Parliament is witness.[4] As Major observes in his essay, parliamentary democracy is still evolving. The 25th edition of Erskine May – the authoritative guide to parliamentary conventions and practice – rolled off the press in 2019, continuing to reflect, not make, the ultimately flexible parliamentary conventions.[5] Parliament depends upon parliamentarians being – to use Peter Hennessy's phrase, itself borrowed from Clive Priestley – 'good chaps',[6] even though being 'good' is not, as has been said, in the job description.

The constitutional principle is that the elected Government of the day – the Executive – is subject to Parliament. Government proposes changes to the law, but it is Parliament that decides.[7] When policies are not controversial, or there is a clear majority of MPs on the Government's side in Parliament, Parliament's scrutiny of the Executive is noisy but straightforward. Government policies are generally carried. But Brexit is not uncontroversial; indeed it is the most controversial issue in British politics since at least the 1930s, and there is at the time of writing no government majority in the House of Commons and scant agreement among those on the government side of the House. In these turbulent years, MPs have experienced major tensions in the many loyalties they owe: to their constituents (divided over Brexit); to their parties (mostly divided over Brexit); to their leaders (with whom they may disagree over Brexit); to the stability of the country (rocked by Brexit); and to their own consciences (often riven by Brexit). There is no possibility of sleepily voting with or against the Government now.

Within this unsteady hinterland of human fallibility, amendable convention, polarising loyalties and a fiendishly difficult task, MPs are under intense pressure to deliver a goal demanded by a referendum that was 'inserted' into our parliamentary system[8] without due thought for the manifold implications of a result that was not government policy at the time. MPs are acting out the pain and division felt across the country, and theirs is the testing privilege of doing so under the pitiless glare of publicity. But this is the essence of our parliamentary democracy: our elected representatives, and no one else, must find a way forward, and they must do so in plain sight. With all their volatile – human – fallibility, we neverthe-less look to the representatives we have chosen to exercise their skill and experience in the best and most responsible way on our behalf. They are not our delegates. It is demanding enough that an MP has to try to win the hearts and minds of their constituents at election time. Once elected, we have to respect the responsibility laid upon them and wait for the next elec-tion to indicate our support, or lack of it, for what they do on our behalf. We should cut our MPs some slack as they strug-gle to find a way through, because the underlying principles of representational democracy and the sovereignty of Parliament are more important than our strongly held views on Brexit. In other words, the means matter – not just the outcome – and defending those means entails compassion, rather than threats of rape and death,[9] for our all-too-human MPs. Otherwise, those who have some virtue and wisdom in them, who might think to stand or remain as MPs, will simply not take the per-sonal, moral and spiritual risk.

The Civil Service

The constitution provides balance to its volatile heart of democracy with a Civil Service that is politically impartial.[10] Unlike many other government administrations around the world, civil servants (with the exception of some ambassadors) are not appointed by politicians but have to apply for and be accepted into the Service on merit.[11] Civil servants uphold the core principle of democracy by enacting the will of the gov-ernment ministers who run their departments, but they are required at the same time to be independent custodians of propriety.[12] The Civil Service Code requires them to exercise the four values of honesty, objectivity, political impartiality and integrity, ensuring that 'public money and other resources are used properly and efficiently'.[13] If their ministers ask them to do something they believe is wrong, they can ask for an 'instruction', which places on record that they do not agree with a proposed use of public money. Ultimately, if there is no other way to resolve a disagreement, they have to resign from the Civil Service.[14]

The Brexit years have coincided with a time of questioning objective truth. There is a great value in this: objective truth is indeed elusive, and those who claim they have it are rarely right. Too much self-confidence can lead to 'groupthink', and the Civil Service is addressing this tendency with a young but active culture of diversity. But the post-modern recognition that there is no such thing as a 'view from nowhere'[15] has been hijacked in the Brexit years by unscrupulous rivals who claim that 'no objective truth' means 'no truth'. Every statement is contestable on this basis: 'you only say that because you are a Leaver/Remainer, and I will not trust a word of it'. 'Post-truth' thinking makes reasonable debate impossible because not only is there no 'view from nowhere' but there is no common view at all. The tendency is exacerbated, though not caused, by the advent of digital technology and social media as they can reinforce prejudices, as Clegg observes.

The fluid moral backwater of our post-truth society, together with pressure to deliver results, gives the four critical values of the Civil Service scant purchase. If civil servants proffer advice that demonstrates the difficulties and disadvantages of a Brexit-related policy, how are they to demonstrate the objectivity of their conclusions? How can they show that they are not – as their political masters, and the public, have been wont to say – simply coming at it with the wrong attitude? If they supported what they were supposed to be bringing about, the argument goes, their advice would be more positive. As one civil servant put it, they feel they are having to prove they are 'true believers' in Brexit.[16] The very notion is anathema to the values of objectivity and political impartiality, but civil servants are humans too. How long would any of us defend such values, fallible humans that we are, if our jobs increasingly depended upon our demonstration of politicised loyalty, riding roughshod over carefully researched and prepared advice? Would we take the nuclear option of resignation, if we had a family to support? But the objectivity and impartiality of the Civil Service, together with its requirement of its officials to be honest and have integrity, are major protections against the volatility of politics. These values sit right at the heart of the British constitution and ensure the functioning of democracy by preventing the harm caused by too-swiftly enacted, unthought-through policies. Even as we recognise that truth is impossible to demonstrate absolutely, we should want our civil servants to strive to come as close to it as they can. Objective truth may be elusive, but that only means we have to dig deeper to find it in the midst of our divided perspectives and complex circumstances.[17]

The Judiciary

The Judiciary also provides support to our democratic system by being independent. Judges are not political appointees, and they administer the laws made by Parliament independent of all political pressures. In practice, this involves a great deal of interpretation of statutory legislation as well as the development of principles derived from common law, but Parliament can change statutes and the process of developing common law is ultimately also subject to Parliament.

When asked to pronounce on the legality of issues that are politically sensitive, judges can find themselves unfairly accused of being politically motivated. This has been most pressingly and harshly the case in their judgements on constitutional matters relating to Brexit: 'Enemies of the People', lambasted the *Daily Mail*[18] after the High Court of England and Wales ruled that, notwithstanding the 'leave' result in the EU referendum, Parliament had to pass a new act before the UK could commence the process of leaving the EU.[19] More recently, the decision by the Supreme Court on the unlawfulness of the 2019 prorogation of Parliament[20] has attracted angry condemnation by some members of the public and parts of the media. The judges have slowed things down by upholding the sovereignty of Parliament so they must be partisan, shout the headlines in words to that effect. The Prime Minister himself said, 'I think that the court was wrong to pronounce on what is essentially a political question.'[21]

The courts have indeed slowed down the process of Brexit by their upholding of the fundamental constitutional principles of the sovereignty of Parliament. But that is not the fault of the courts. If there were not such a divided Parliament, the judgements would not have slowed the process down. What the courts have done is to ensure that no damage is done to the constitution (so far) in the journey to Brexit. Their concern is with the means (the acts done to achieve Brexit), not the end (Brexit itself). This has highlighted another profound difference of view running through the Brexit years, which is that some will think the ends justify the means, and some will not. The EU referendum was decisive, so Brexit must be attained by any means, argues the former view. The latter argues that the EU referendum may have been decisive, but the goal of Brexit – like any goal – must be reached through morally justifiable acts. The former view will argue that any act that brings about Brexit will be morally right because the goal is morally right. The latter view will say that some actions are morally wrong, even if they bring about an outcome that is morally right.

The pressure to achieve a goal can be very great, seemingly justifying any and all means required, especially if it is taking a very long time. The Judiciary has shown itself to be robust in the face of loud criticisms; they are surviving the stress test so far, but the toll it takes should not be underestimated. Unlike the anonymity of all but the most senior civil servants, judges' names sit beside their judgements for all time. You are named and your photograph is published on the front page of the newspaper that accuses you of treachery. No doubt the judges involved are receiving their share of death threats. If we do not understand and cherish the inestimable value of having an independent judiciary, we may start descending down the slippery slope of politically appointed judges for whom the distinction between process and outcome may not be so clear.

In defence of slow power
The balance of power sown into the British constitution has made nothing about the process of Brexit straightforward. But that is as it should be. We, the electorate, should not want

as complex a policy as leaving the EU to go through on the nod. We should want our elected representatives to express the deep disquiet the people in general feel. We should realise that time is needed to ease ourselves out of hardened positions into places of compromise, because some of the compromises – such as the Irish border and the challenge of forging new trade deals around the world – require deep roots to be dug up, strong branches to be sawn off, finely tuned relationships to be ended and new courtships begun. We should want our civil servants to be looking at the detail – the devil is always in the detail – of what the departure means, allowing them to articulate without fear the challenges that have to be overcome. We should want our Judiciary to ensure that our constitution is protected as we work our way out against the tremendous, growing pressure just to do it, finish it, stop the painful arguments, the complicated, confounding concerns and more or less scrupulous uses of parliamentary convention to gain political advantage.

Such attention to the detailed consequences of a profound shift in our international alliances and modes of working means that Brexit has taken, and will continue to take, a long time. It is undoubtedly frustrating. Even the slow, constitutionally bound evolution of a new, post-Brexit way of being in the world is taken to be self-interested foot-dragging by the establishment in order to prevent Brexit from happening at all.

The moral evolution of 'the establishment'
The balance of power between the Legislature, the Judiciary and the Executive – so neatly laid out on three sides of Parliament Square if one stands with Westminster Abbey at one's

back[22] and with loyalty owed and sworn to the Crown (which has, in practice, no direct power of its own) – has protected the nation well against the draw of tyranny, to which unrestrained populism can succumb. Westminster Abbey Institute has argued many times in favour of ensuring healthy institutions as a means of safeguarding good governance, since no individual can be relied upon to succeed in such a weighty obligation alone, and nor can they rely upon followers who remain loyal.[23] To cite Benjamin Disraeli, 'Individuals may form communities, but it is institutions alone that can create a nation'.[24] But our post-modern minds, questioning objective truth, argue that Westminster Abbey Institute would be expected to put forward such a case because it is itself an ancient institution bound to the traditional establishment. Along with the institutions of public service who are our neighbours and are nearly as old as we are, the Abbey has been, and certainly has been viewed as, accessible only to a few. We are believed to be unaware of the reality of life for the many.

The self-confidence of the establishment, already dealing with wholesale loss of deference, has been further shaken by the Brexit referendum and the voices that have been heard in its wake, voices of angry protest at having been ignored or forgotten or misunderstood. Perhaps a brilliant leader, who at least claims to know what life is like for the ordinary person, would clear the path either to overthrow or significantly reform our institutions in ways that their slow evolution and their strictest adherents will never countenance. Not all populists are bad, as Clegg points out. In the midst of the frustratingly slow enactment of the EU referendum result, buccaneering politics can be utterly refreshing. The popular, energetic, forceful and irresistible leader can move in to make a thing happen by the sheer force of their will.

We should be warned, however. Writing at the beginning of the twentieth century, Max Weber anticipated the characteristics of the charismatic leaders of our times, so there is nothing new here: first, 'their power rests on beating rivals in competition rather than knowledge or the right of inheritance'; second, they articulate and defend a new direction and new values for the country that originate from creative individuals, not from institutions; and third, they declare not institutions but themselves personally responsible for their policies.[25] If these are to be the characteristics of the leaders of our future years, then our constitutional institutions are seriously threatened – not, in all likelihood, by some quick coup, but slowly, as their moral stuffing is neglected, their service misunderstood and their meaning lost.

Rather than tear down the temple, or dismantle it brick by brick, we would be better to continue more strenuously to attend to its moral evolution. Westminster Abbey Institute seeks to support this task, drawing upon its deep Christian roots, envisioning leadership as service, offering its neighbours the opportunity to take time to reflect on the good they are trying to do for the public.[26] A Christian perspective turns service itself upside down by placing the poor and vulnerable, including our vulnerable planet, at its heart. The rich and clever and strong have much to learn from the weak, as Jean Vanier showed with his L'Arche movement[27] and Angus Ritchie has recently urged.[28]

Aspirational democracy

In an argument that refreshingly proposes the opposite of the well-known Churchillian suggestion that democracy is the worst form of government except for all the others,[29] quoted by Major in his essay, Costica Bradatan argues by contrast that 'democracy is for the gods'. It is, Bradatan suggests, a form of perfection that no human society can hope to attain, though we should constantly try, for democracy is no less than the assurance that all members of society 'should have an equal say in how we conduct our lives together'.[30] Democracy is an aspiration because it requires humility: we must each of us know that I am no better than any of the others.

Major asked the audience at his 2017 lecture whether anyone thought our 850-year-old democracy was perfect; not one hand was raised. It is a journey, not a destination. And, he argues, it is not simply about winning elections. The trappings of democracy are not to be mistaken for democracy's purpose. It is for the government, he says, of all those who can be seen and also those who cannot be seen: future generations, the losers in elections, political opponents, the country itself, the international community. And all governments, he says, 'have a responsibility to themselves for the manner in which they govern'.

Perhaps the outcome of these difficult times will be a written constitution, different institutions of government or a series of popular leaders who bind themselves to the people, not to any structure. But from Westminster Abbey's long-term perspective, such changes do not in themselves change humans. The troubles we are facing are caused by human error, or rather, to put it more accurately as well as more kindly, fallible human attempts to get it right. Changing externalities won't change us. We still have to attend to our own virtue, our moral character, our willingness to walk around in the skins of others as much as we can, as Atticus teaches Scout.[31] The aspiration of a truly democratic society is a good one if, as Bradatan says, it results in a recognition of our common fallibility and our need to accommodate each other and compromise. Both Major and Clegg urge this view, and their essays merit careful reading.

The Responsibilities of Democracy

The Rt Hon Sir John Major

As a boy in the 1950s, encouraged by two very impudent close friends, I cut my teeth as a public speaker on a soapbox, across the river in Brixton Market and, in those early days, I guess none of my friends would have imagined that one day my soapbox would be upgraded to a lectern in this beautiful and historic Abbey. I doubt, those years ago, that I imparted very much wisdom from my Brixton soapbox, but I did learn about people. No one barracked. No one told me in Brixton Market, as surely they could have done, to go away and come back when I knew something about, well, anything. Even in a crowded and busy market, people took time to stop and listen or question. No one seemed to resent me or my views, nor were they hostile, although many must have disagreed with what I said. Today, as politics has become more rancorous, I have often thought back to that time and wondered how we lost that tolerance of opposing views. Certainly, that tolerance was missing from the 2016 EU referendum campaign, when honest and thoughtful political debate was, from time to time, abandoned in favour of exaggeration, half-truths and untruths, and no one seemed either ashamed or embarrassed by this. Indeed, some revelled in it. This suggests that mendacity is acceptable, providing it panders to a popular prejudice. Such lies are then sanctioned by many who know them to be untrue and welcomed by others whose prejudices are supported by them. And if they are delivered with wit and panache, they may even be believed. Some of the media reported what was said, even when they must have known it to be improbable at best or untrue at worst and, in that way, the EU referendum showcased a deterioration in both the conduct and reporting of our politics.

There will be those who think that my subject, 'the responsibilities of democracy', is inappropriate for Westminster Abbey because it is a secular concern. The arts and practice of democratic politics are far removed from the higher concerns of the Church. They are wrong – as wrong, or as misguided, as those who argue that the Church should stay out of politics. It should not. Both the Church and state care for the well-being of people and, if one institution is failing them, then the other has a duty to say so. Two-way constructive criticism, if conducted civilly, is healthy and no one should shrink from it. In years gone by, the Church was sometimes criticised as 'the Tory party at prayer'. Today, it is often told it is too left-wing. I doubt the first was ever true, and the charge of left-wing bias is trotted out whenever the Church talks about poverty. But the Church *should* talk about poverty. So should we all. Indeed, poverty has never been the sole preserve of the left: conservatives from William Wilberforce to David Cameron, who made overseas aid to the very poorest a signature policy, have focused upon poverty.

On occasions such as this, there are two kinds of lecture. One is uplifting and intellectual; it enlivens the conscience and leaves us pondering the higher purpose of humankind. The other, of which mine is one, has a more prosaic purpose. My lecture seeks to provoke thought about democracy, both generally and in our own country. Democracy is very precious, but how is it performing in a new world that is changing at bewildering speed? Is it doing its job? Is it at risk? Where is it failing? What is its future? In many countries today I see a distaste for politics that runs very deep. That is a danger to democracy. So inevitably my theme this evening is, in part, a cry for action where there is none and of warning where there is peril.

What is democracy? It is surely more than electing a government through a universal franchise. Elections are an expression of democracy, but the ballot box alone is insufficient. President Putin wins elections: is Russia a democracy? No, it is not. Is Turkey? Is Egypt? Even on the narrowest and meanest of definitions, the answer is no, and the same is true for many other countries that hold elections, some of which are rigged. Voting apart, these countries have few of the attributes of a genuine democracy.

My worry, my concern, is that democracy is in retreat: stifled in part by its own virtues. Democracy operates on consent. That being so, it is slower to make decisions than autocracy or outright dictatorship. Democracy must cajole, persuade and seek consensus. Not so autocracy. And this can make autocracy seem much more efficient than democracy, more decisive, more able to deliver its promises, more prompt to act in a time of crisis. The rise of non-democratic China to economic superstardom is one of the great stories of history, but there is a price to pay for her success and that price is a lack of personal freedom for the masses. For now, no doubt countless Chinese people are grateful for the economic improvement, but human nature suggests that, as their individual wellbeing grows, they will demand greater personal choice and liberty, and, if that happens – when that happens – autocracy must yield or repress. The same choice lies ahead for many countries.

At the heart of true democracy is liberty: liberty under the law. Democratic government must be freely elected for a fixed period in a universal franchise, untainted by coercion. There must be checks and balances to its authority. The rule of law must apply, even to the most powerful. The Judiciary must be independent, and there must be a free media, an independent academia and a functioning opposition, free to oppose without sanctions. Only then can freedom of speech and action be protected. But these attributes, even *these* attributes, are merely the trappings of democracy.

Democracy in action is more than satisfying the material demands of the majority or honouring the promises of an election manifesto. It seems to me that democratic government must govern for the future as well as the present. A governing party must govern for political opponents who did not vote for them and may never do so. It must govern for the unborn and the country they will inherit; it must govern for minorities and for the wider international community; and all governments have a responsibility to themselves for the manner in which they govern.

One has only to set out these responsibilities to see that no government, perhaps ever, has met this ideal. Government by humans, not saints, is not a vehicle for perfection. But that does not mean the imperfections of governments should be ignored or accepted. Yet today, in some parts of the world, they often are, as a disillusioned, uninterested, preoccupied or, in some cases, a cowed or misled electorate shrug their shoulders and turn away. In such a climate, there is a risk that democracy faces a threat from the rise of nationalism. This is not a theoretical threat: in many countries, it is a reality. In others, it is a clear and present danger.

In the democratic West, we have come to believe that our liberal social and economic model of democracy is unchallengeable. It is not. In 2016, as the United Nations has reported,[32] 67 countries suffered a decline in political and civil liberties while only 36 had gains. What has happened in these countries can happen elsewhere. Over 20 democracies have collapsed since the mid-1990s and, as we all know, there is widespread dissatisfaction in many others.

Across Europe, our own backyard, nationalism has gained more than a foothold. It begins with a populism that masquerades as patriotism but morphs into something far less attractive. In many countries, nationalist parties have significant support. They can attract true patriots, but they are also a political vehicle for those who flavour that patriotism with xenophobia. Nationalism is authoritarian. It turns easily towards autocracy or, at worst, outright dictatorship. Nationalists hide their threat under an exaggerated love of a country, an unthinking patriotism: 'my country, right or wrong'. Its leaders view other countries, and sometimes other races, as inferior. Nationalism is suspicious of foreigners. It accuses immigrants of 'stealing jobs' or in some other way undermining the 'indigenous' population. This has been so for hundreds of years. It is often wrong and, let it be said in this House of God, un-Christian.

There is an immense divide between nationalism and patriotism. Patriotism is more than pride in a country. A mature patriotism concerns itself with the condition of the people, as well as the prestige of the nation. Such a patriotism worries about deprivation, about opportunity, and about incentive, and it asks itself, 'How can we spread our wealth and opportunity more evenly around our country?' It is as concerned with the growth of foodbanks as it is with any shortage of aircraft carriers.

I fear for the loss of our broad, socially liberal attitudes. The financial crisis of 2007 and onwards led to less security, low or no growth and rising taxes, and that has created public dissatisfaction with the old, albeit fallible, politics. Anger about its shortcomings replaces cool, dispassionate judgement about its performance. Despair gives a credibility to promises of easy solutions when, in truth, there is none. Our social and economic liberalism may be fallible, but it is not some mishmash of woolly headed do-gooders. It protects individual liberties and human rights, promotes market freedoms, ownership of property and freedom of movement. We dare not take these values, so familiar to us, for granted. We need to celebrate them, protect them and practise them. Politics must not become a playground for demagogues. Capitalism and free trade, in my view, are bulwarks of democracy. They have lifted untold millions of the poorest people in the world out of abject poverty. As trade has grown, wealth has grown. As wealth has grown, money has been spent, literacy levels have risen and fatal diseases have been eradicated. But free trade is under attack. When growth was buoyant, all was well but, after the financial crash, many workers around the world see global trade as a threat. They are told to see it as a threat, and many companies exposed to foreign competition feel the same way.

Now, there are problems here that have to be addressed. Globalism has been a force for good, but it has distributed its gains very unevenly. Individuals have gained wealth that Croesus would have envied. Global companies have driven out competitors and become mega rich. To protect itself, capitalism must be ethical and, if it is not, then opposition to it will grow. So business must confront malpractice and eliminate it. Capitalism must reform itself or government must do so for it. 'Anything goes' capitalism is not acceptable: it can only damage free trade and open markets and encourage protectionism, less trade, slower growth and, as a result, greater poverty. If that happens, everyone loses, but those with the least will lose the most.

Around the world, our British democracy is seen as honest, not corrupt, free, not repressive. Our legal system is widely admired and respected. Our elections are acknowledged as fair, not fixed; governments leave and enter office without violence, and they do so within a few days. Our Parliament has been a democratic model. As a nation we can, and should, be proud of all this and I am – with reservations.

Let me say, first, that I have never been among that minority of Britons who disparage our country and always side with its critics. I am, and I always will be, proud to be British. But, having seen our democracy at work over many years from the inside and for many years from the outside as a reasonably informed observer, not all is as it could be, or should be. We can do better. Our present Parliament faces an extraordinary range of complex problems. Brexit – a historic blunder in my own view, though it is not my theme for this lecture – will consume the time of this Parliament and crowd out domestic issues that are crying out for action and have done for a long time. It cannot be, but it would be better were Parliament free to focus its attention on health, on social care, on housing, on education, on transport and on deprivation. But until Brexit has been resolved, which may take years, few – if any – of these subjects will get the full attention that they merit. Nor will constitutional issues over Scotland or Northern Ireland, or the social problems of income disparity and the North–South divide, which surely cannot be permitted to continue as it is. All of these, each of them vital to the wellbeing of our country, will be secondary to the fallout from the EU referendum.

On the day I entered Downing Street in 1990, I set out an ambition to produce a country at ease with itself. For a raft of reasons I failed in that and no one has subsequently succeeded, but that objective is as important today as it was when I set it out over a quarter of a century ago.

As I said, I have reservations. To cynics, the words 'service' and 'duty' are old-fashioned, yet they are virtues that deserve praise, not scorn. To a very large extent, our public service embodies them. The Civil Service is a fundamental engine of our democracy. It has a historic memory, which protects against the errors of the past being repeated. It is politically independent. It brings balance to our system of government and yet, in the last 20 years, it has been undermined by its own political masters. When things have gone wrong, a small number of ministers, against all past practice, have blamed the Civil Service for the failure and not themselves. Political special advisers have undermined civil servants and usurped their role. The Freedom of Information Act has hampered the dispassionate advice offered to ministers because, in due course, it will be published and civil servants are not public figures in the sense that the latter's views are expected to be made public. Ministers may decide policy, but the Civil Service must deliver it and, to do so, it trawls for ideas, delves deep into potential pitfalls, advises, cautions and prepares legislation. It is, very much, in our national interest that public service should remain a career that attracts some of the very best brains in our country. We should value it, not disparage it, and I hope that the Government will rethink some recent approaches towards special advisers. Ministers have a right to non-Civil Service advice but, as advisers are paid from the public purse, they should, I believe, be people of experience and ability. Many are, but not all. Their role needs refining. Good special advisers, with expertise and political nous, can make for better government and better liaison with the Civil Service but, over the years, a handful of advisers have acquired unjustified power that they have misused. At times, they have driven wedges between ministers and their civil servants. Some have been used as attack dogs against both their master's political opponents and colleagues. The culprits were often protected by ministers when they should have been dismissed without ceremony. Some advisers, with intellect but little judgement, are easy prey for the media. They are flattered, wined and dined, and the naive among them talk unguardedly while the more unscrupulous leak stories – perhaps under orders – that create feuds between senior ministers and complicate policy. This is not what special advisers are appointed for. Any that behave in this fashion should go. A 'one leak and you're out' policy would be a worthwhile discipline for the Prime Minister to institute across all government departments.

It is a strength of our democracy that debate on policy is fierce. That is as it should be; policy affects people's lives. Passions can rise, and sometimes it is right that they do so, but policy disagreement is not only heard across the floor of Parliament. Too often, members of the same party are seen as opponents – not 'one of us', to echo an unfortunate phrase from the 1980s[33] – and this leads to rival camps being formed. And these factions, opposing wings of the same party, fight one another more vigorously than they do their opponents. This is potentially destructive of the party system, which is the main operating structure of our democracy. The old political adage 'my opponents are opposite, my enemies are behind' is currently apt for both our main parties, and there is a reason for this. The anti-European right wish to control the Conservative Party; the neo-Marxist left wish to dominate the Labour Party. Both are making headway in a battle for the soul of their respective political parties. But these ideological battles have dangers for our democracy. The rebellious radicals of right and left argue for partisan policies that appeal to the extremes of their party base. And as they do so, political divisions widen, consensus shrinks and a minority of the party begins to manipulate the majority. This is dangerous territory. The malcontents would be wise to remember that, without some give and take, without some effort at consensus, our tolerant party system can become ungovernable. In politics, as in life, consensus is wise not weak, and tolerance is a virtue not a failing. If fringes begin to dominate a political party, I believe the middle ground of their support will turn away in disgust, and the shrillest voices and the most extreme views will begin to dominate debate. Where that risk arises, democrats should worry. Indeed, they should do more than worry: they should fight back.

Politics has always been a rough trade. It arouses strong feelings and plain speaking, which, sometimes, can turn into abuse. A hard-boiled professional will say, 'If you can't stand the heat, get out of the kitchen'. Well, maybe, but the language and tone of politics matters. It can enthuse or repel, excite or deflate, uplift or cast down. Clarify or confuse. It can examine the truth or ignore it. In the 1930s, the fascist leader Oswald Mosley used his oratory to stir up violence. During World War II, Churchill, in Ed Murrow's memorable phrase, 'mobilised the English language and sent it to war'. In the 1960s, the Conservative Enoch Powell inflamed opinion on immigration, and the dockers marched in his support. Oratory can change public opinion for good or for ill, and today we need it to explain increasingly complex policy in a way that is readily understood.

The world is different today from the way it was. It has decayed since the popular press fully reported speeches in Parliament. The speeches may have been dry, even dull, but perhaps by osmosis, policy was understood. It is more difficult now. Today's world is more complex, policy is more complex and today's media world is much more complex. We cannot expect the written press to act as a public service. It is losing readership and fighting for its very existence. In its struggle for survival, it favours sensation, because sensation is more likely to sell newspapers. This entertains, but it may not necessarily inform. Many political stories – you will all have read them – are spiced up by 'informed sources'. Such stories are often self-interested, malicious comment and should be read with many a pinch of salt. It may excite and intrigue, but it rarely leaves people very much wiser. Television news is more informative but not always so. Often interviews are brief and confrontational and focused on securing a headline for the next news bulletin. Political news programmes have longer interviews and can be a better source of information but they, too, often slip into confrontation. In each of the above charades, the electorate is left perhaps confused and, almost certainly, uninformed.

We cannot only blame the media. Spin and soundbite were political inventions. They replaced argument with meaningless phrases: Labour's 'tough on crime, tough on the causes of crime' and the Conservative's 'take back control' serve as memorable examples of pitch-perfect absurdity. They convey nothing, they explain nothing and they are worth nothing. And they can mislead, as I have discovered: I once used the phrase 'back to basics' and it was taken up to pervert a thoroughly worthwhile social policy, persuading people it was about something quite different.[34] And the low point was reached when politicians were offered a daily 'form of words' by their parties to be trotted out in every interview. This is not only undignified, it is self-defeating. As voters hear our elected representatives uttering puerile slogans instead of explaining policy, it is no wonder, is it, if respect melts away? Slogans and soundbites are a deceit. Electors deserve the truth in plain English, not in fairytales. When trust in our elected representative falls, democracy fails.

Now there are, I concede, rare occasions when public interest demands politicians to be, as the phrase goes, 'economical with the truth' but, in the main, clarity and honesty really are the best policy. And by honesty, I mean more than simply straight talking. I mean honesty in facing up to challenges, honesty in acknowledging fears and dangers and difficulties, honesty in action, honesty in admitting there are limitations to what any government can do. Honesty can be very politically inconvenient, but less so than concealing the truth. Honesty commands respect. Slogans and soundbites do not. Spin certainly does not. Honesty is essential in a functioning democracy. It is infuriating to listen to interviews in which every question is sidestepped or answered with obfuscation. Such conduct treats the electorate with contempt, and no one should be surprised if they return the compliment. I do not wish to be prissy about this and appear to suggest there was some past, mythical age in which everything was perfect. If there was, I have never heard of it; I was certainly never part of it. But politicians can do better to serve the electorate and I think, at this moment, it would be a very good idea for them to do so.

The essence of our democracy is 'one person, one vote'. However, except in the ballot box, no democracy in truth offers equal influence to every citizen. Anthony Trollope, in his biography of Cicero, observed that the power of voting was common to all citizens, but the power of influencing the electors had passed into the hands of the rich.[35] Now that was, of course, two millennia ago in Ancient Rome, but the same power of influencing – not remotely to the same extent – lingers in some modern democracies. The very rich, if they assert themselves, may be able to influence government. In America (I speak as someone who is one-quarter American) big money perverts the system. The sheer cost of their elections, with most of the money spent on advertisements attacking their opponents, is enormous. A member of Congress seeking election every two years is perpetually fundraising. No wonder they do not have passports and do not go abroad. Even if donors ask nothing in return for their generosity, that generosity is likely to be in the mind of the politician as they consider policy, and it ought not to be. In the UK, we are luckier: money is far less damaging to our system, but it still manifests itself through party funding. Party funding is an acute dilemma. All political parties must raise money to campaign, to run their organisations, to pay their staff, and none can hope to fund this through membership subscriptions alone. There are only two ways to fund the balance, and neither is attractive. At present, the bulk of funding is by wealthy individuals, business and the trade unions. This is bound to give rise to obligations, whether sought or not sought by the donor, and is intrinsically unhealthy. In my experience, many donors are altruistic and give money simply because they wish to support the party of their choice, but some may seek to exact a price. Whether that price is a policy promise, an appointment or an honour, it is undesirable. An alternative is more funding through the public purse. This would be deeply unpopular with the electorate and I share the general distaste for it. Nonetheless, democratically, it may be the least bad option. A compromise might be more state funding than at present but, in return, a legal limit on donations from individuals or businesses or trade unions: a legal limit that should be set at a level where nobody could subsequently reasonably argue that it influences policy or buys reward. Such a scheme is not perfect and it is certainly unpopular but, on balance, I believe it would be beneficial for our democratic system.

Here tonight, in this magnificent and hallowed place, we are surrounded by the spirits of many historical figures who were elected over the ages to represent us – over many centuries, many generations – through times of strife and turmoil, times of uncertainty and change, times of national crisis and times of celebration. They are commemorated here for the service that they gave in their lifetime to our nation. Whatever their political beliefs, they were all elected by the people to serve the people, and it was the people who had the power to dismiss them.

As a boy, I read Edmund Burke. Let me quote him now:

> To deliver an opinion is the right of all men; that of constituents is a weighty and respectable opinion, which a representative ought always to rejoice to hear; and which he ought always most seriously to consider. But *authoritative* instructions, *mandates* issued, which the member is bound blindly and implicitly to obey, to vote, and to argue for, though contrary to the clearest conviction of his judgement and conscience; these are things utterly unknown to the laws of this land, and which arise from a fundamental mistake of the whole order and tenor of our constitution.[36]

I agree with that Burke quotation, without qualification.

As that young boy across the river, 60-odd years ago, I would never have anticipated that the weight of that responsibility would ever fall upon my own shoulders. It was a privilege, but a burden too, as it is for all who bear it. And all must ask themselves, 'Did I do what I believed to be right? Did I speak up, not afraid to speak the truth?' We are blessed to live in this land, but each and every one of us has a responsibility to keep democracy alive and fresh and kicking and never stifle free speech or freedom of action, provided it is within the law. Earlier, I spoke of my soapbox in Brixton and the tolerance that was shown to me in the salad days of my young political life by many who could quite reasonably have taken a very different view from mine. 'I do not like what you say,' said Voltaire, 'but I will defend to the death your right to say it'.[37] Indeed so. That is the responsibility of democracy.

The Very Reverend Dr John Hall
It has taken 850 years since the Conquest for full democracy to evolve in Britain. What is the global story? Do you have hopes, expectations, that democracy will ultimately be the manner of government, of rule, in every nation?

Sir John Major
I think there is a difficulty here. You mentioned it has taken 850 years for us to develop our democracy. Hands up all those who think our democracy is perfect [not one hand was raised]. Exactly. After 850 years, it isn't. So the belief that we can pick up our democracy and transplant it into other countries where they have no historical instinct for democracy, where they have a different culture, is fatuous: it isn't going to happen. People will build up to their own form of democracy in their own

way, and it is arrogant of us to think that we can artificially transplant our democracy to other countries. If they seek our help, we can provide them with the background to how our democracy works, with the need for a Civil Service, with what the trappings of democracy are and with what its practice should actually be. But for us to try and implant it elsewhere is a mistake. Will it grow in other countries? I think, over time, it will because, as in the example I gave earlier, when a country is very poor, if a government comes along – of whatever nature – and begins to improve the quality of life for those people, they are grateful, but human nature never stays grateful forever. The Church hasn't worked that out yet. As people become more self-dependent and better off, they demand more, and in countries where there isn't freedom of choice and freedom of action that is what they are likely to demand. So, it will build up in countries over time, and I think there will be more. Churchill once said, 'Democracy is the worst form of government, except for all those other forms that have been tried from time to time',[38] and I don't think that phrase will ever be bettered. So, yes, democracy will evolve elsewhere on the globe, but it will be self-generating: it will not be inflicted upon people by us.

Audience member

Sixty years ago, Harold Macmillan made his speech 'Wind of Change'[39] in which he announced the end of colonisation. Do you think, 60 years on, we're going through a new 'wind of change' and if so, how would you describe it?

Sir John Major

Macmillan's 'Wind of Change' speech was not much remarked on in South Africa when he made it. It was only later that people realised what he said. His speech presaged a good degree of decolonisation. We don't have colonies to lose now, but we are living through a time of unprecedented change. There are winds of change of all sorts. If anybody had asked us three years ago, who would have forecast what has happened in America, in Britain, in Europe or in many other parts of the world over the last two or three years? And change is accelerating. Not only change in politics but change in every sphere of life. Some of this change is very good. There are many people who are alive today because of the changes in medicine that have been so effective over the last few decades. Developments in science more generally are changing many of the ways in which we live. There are going to be changes in robotics and artificial intelligence that will alter the future world of work and, as a result of that, will alter the nature of education because we are going to have to educate our young generations to be equipped for the new world of work. So it's not a wind of change in one area that we're facing; it's a hurricane of change from almost every side. It's bewildering because change moves faster than politics possibly can do. I don't think there has ever been a time, in peacetime, where it has been more difficult to be a politician than it is at the present moment because of the sheer scale and speed of change and the challenge of coping with the public demand for an instant response. We live in a world of instant demands and the expectation of an instant response to those demands, and those can't always be met. So the change is quite extraordinary and dramatic.

Audience member

As a statesman who has contributed so much towards the establishment of peace and democratic processes in Northern Ireland, do you think that the problems that may flow from Brexit, in the wake of Brexit, may present particular problems in that area?

Sir John Major

Northern Ireland in 1990, when the peace process began, was a very different place from Northern Ireland after the negotiations, after the signing of the Easter Agreement. It was not only different within Northern Ireland; it was different on the island of Ireland. The relationship between north and south is better than it has been at any time since partition, and the relationship between Dublin and London has been better, in the last few years, than it has been at any time in the long history of the United Kingdom and Ireland. And, if we get a border between Northern Ireland and the south as a result of Brexit, it is going to cause a huge amount of disruption. The aim of the EU, and of the Northern Irish Government, and of the British Government, is to minimise any disruption, and everybody is prepared to work together to that end. But it is very difficult to see how we can avoid a border of some sort. The sheer scale of trade that goes from south to north is extraordinary. There is over two hundred billion pounds worth of trade coming from Ireland into the UK every day. If there were to be checks at the border, about two thousand lorries would be affected every day, and all sorts of foodstuffs that can't be dealt with electronically would have to be physically examined as they passed across. There are a great many things made in the Republic of Ireland that are packaged or treated in the north, for example Guinness, which is made in the Republic then transported to Belfast to be bottled. And there are many people in the north and in the south who make things out of a whole range of different components, some of which are in the north, some of which are in the south, and they're going backwards and forwards, like yo-yos, dropping them off and picking them up. It is going to be extraordinarily difficult, and I very much hope we may be able to find a way of avoiding a border. You could, of course, do it if you stayed in the customs union; that would avoid the border. You could do it if you stayed in the single market in the customs union; that too would avoid it. But if you don't, there is going to be a border and the question will be how frictionless could it be? The free movement of people between the Republic and the UK we can deal with – that's not a difficult problem. Free movement of goods is much more complex.

Audience member
I would like to ask you more about the habits that feed into political culture, which you touched upon in your lecture. More than 50 years ago I worked on the Devlin Report on the Nyasaland state of emergency.[40] It was in Macmillan's time, and he managed to persuade the chairman of that commission of enquiry not to include an executive summary. That was something your own government did with the Scott Inquiry.[41] But there was more coverage of government and parliamentary affairs in the *Daily Express* in 1959, when my report came out, than there was in the *Daily Telegraph* in 1995 when yours came out. That's an example of a big shift in political habits

and political discourse between those two dates. Hansard, at one time, was a voluntary thing that was resisted by the political class. Do you see any cause for optimism, in terms of those habits that feed a political culture, that help create a healthy political system?

Sir John Major

You're quite right about the weight of the practical detail of politics in the press. It's a different world now and it's an oddity, isn't it? We have more media than we've ever had before. We have social media on a scale no one dreamed of in 1959 – or even, probably, in 1989 – and yet it is dominated by things other than the practical information that helps people make up their mind about politics. But it's not just the media that have changed; the mass membership of the political parties is different now. The Labour Party had a great influx of young people at the time of the 2017 general election – though I understand, from my friends in the Labour Party, that some of them are now disappearing. But the membership of the large political parties used to be a mass membership and it is no longer, and that is not just the failings of the political parties: there wasn't nearly so much to *do* in 1959 as there was in 2015. There are many people of my acquaintance who would never have married had it not been for the political parties in 1959. It is a different world. So I am not sure how you correct that, but it is why, I think, we do need to take seriously how we disseminate fact. Not political oratory, but cold, hard fact about what the implications are of the legislation that we pass, and I don't know of any easy solution. One of the advantages of no longer being in politics is that I don't have to pretend there is an answer to every problem. There isn't and if there is an answer to this one, I'm afraid I don't know it.

Audience member

In 2015, I stood as Labour's parliamentary candidate in my home constituency of Tonbridge and Malling, which is one of the safest Conservative seats in the country, and the experience made me acutely aware of the ways in which 'first past the post' is undermining the quality of our democracy. I had people on the doorstep saying, 'This is the first time I've been canvassed for 40 years and I've lived here all my life'. Others said, 'I would love to vote for Labour or the Liberal Democrats but, in this neck of the woods, is it really worth it?' Is now the time for proportional representation?

Sir John Major

There is an argument for proportional representation and, were I a Liberal, I would undoubtedly advocate it very strongly. There is a disadvantage with it as well that we have to weigh carefully. Take Germany: it has the strongest economy, it is the largest and most important economic and political nation in Europe, and yet it has just had an election [in September 2017] in which a large number of people, of very extreme views, have got into their Parliament precisely because of the proportional representation system. There are in the German Parliament, I think, 94 members of the *Alternative für Deutschland* on the extreme far right and, on the extreme left, *Die Linke* has 69 seats. That is going to complicate policy for Germany, which affects all Europe to a very great extent. Now, there are many deficiencies with first past the post, I don't deny that for a single second but, I think, we have to choose between which set of deficiencies we want. Some of the advantages brought forward by both parties in the last century might not have happened if there weren't a clear majority in the House of Commons. You have to weigh that certainty of being able to deliver policy against the democratic desirability of everybody being able to vote and all sorts of opinions being represented. There isn't a consensus on it, and I very much doubt there ever would be. I don't dismiss the case for proportional representation, but I'm not especially attracted to it for that reason and only that reason.

Audience member
You referred to the fact that inaccuracies and sometimes falsehoods have featured on the political landscape in recent years. To what extent do you think that accountability has featured in our democracy in the last decade? Do you think we've had enough and, if not, do you have any suggestions as to how it might be made a more prominent feature?

Sir John Major
It is very difficult to hold people accountable for telling porkies unless it is pointed out publicly and repeatedly that what someone has said is untrue. Now, that would be quite an occupation for someone, but I do think it's important that statements are called out when they are blatantly untrue. There are some things that are a matter of opinion and fair enough; people have different opinions. But there are some things that are just plain factually wrong. I've been very pleased to see the Office of National Statistics, for example,

say publicly that certain statements are wrong, and I think we must encourage public bodies and the Government to do that. It's within the memory of a number of the parliamentarians whom I see scattered around here that, if you actually lied to the House of Commons, you would cease to be a minister and you might even cease to be a member. Now, maybe we took that too far because sometimes people made a mistake rather than lied, but it's not a bad idea to have a sanction for people in public life who deliberately mislead. And I would like that sanction to be a clear and public acknowledgement, by people who are in a position to know the truth, that what has been said is wrong. I would hope that might begin to change the habits of the minority of people – and it is a small minority of people – who deliberately falsify. People can make mistakes, and they often do, but I don't think there are a vast number who deliberately falsify, though there certainly are some.

Audience member

Sir John, you talked about the risk of easy soundbites and puerile slogans. Where and how do you think we should start being more honest and perhaps, significantly, *who* do you think should start with that honesty?

Sir John Major

I suppose if you find people who are existing on soundbites and puerile slogans, one sanction would be not to vote for them. Another sanction would be, if you are in their constituency, to go and see them and ask, 'What does this mean? Why are you saying this when it is absolutely meaningless? I want to know what clause 71 of the Dustbins Bill really means, and you're not telling me.' Confront them. Unless there is a general demand for much clearer exposition of what is actually happening, then soundbites and puerile slogans are only going to increase. I hope there will be a general demand for clarity. In the 2015 election, I spoke at a large number of marginal seats and many of the young men and women I spoke for were elected. I have to say, I thought they were the best intake that I had seen since 1979, to take an intake purely at random, and I think that is very encouraging because many of them are very high ability – not just the Conservative's intake but also the Labour Party's. So maybe there is some hope. All things are fads and fashions: spin, soundbites and slogans have been a fad and fashion and maybe they will fade. I hope so, but where they don't, we should confront the people who make them.

The Very Reverend Dr John Hall

Once a politician, always a politician. We've heard a wise politician reflecting on his own experience and we're immensely grateful for the provocations and suggestions for improvements. Sir John, thank you for your time, for your wisdom and for the breadth of the discussion you've opened up for us.

The Coarsening of Political Language

The Rt Hon Sir Nicholas Clegg

Coarse political language has been with us since the dawn of political debate: vitriolic, vituperative and shrill. In Ancient Rome, Petronius said to one of his opponents, 'All you do is run back and forth with a stupid expression, jittery as a rat in a roasting pot'.[42] Plautus said, 'Everything you say is so unbearably boring, by Hercules, that it's murder by monotony'.[43] Disraeli, on the difference between misfortune and calamities, is credited with one of my favourites (notwithstanding that he said it about one of my heroes, Gladstone), 'If Gladstone fell into the Thames, that would be misfortune, and if anyone pulled him out, that, I suppose, would be a calamity'. Churchill is famously said to have observed of Attlee that he was, 'A modest man with much to be modest about'. And David Lloyd George reportedly said of Sir John Simon, 'The Right Honourable and learned gentleman has twice crossed the floor of this house, each time leaving behind a trail of slime'. Creative insults and personal abuse are not new.

Nor, for that matter, is the allegation that politicians don't always match their rhetoric with their actions. When politicians indulge in the poetry and aspiration of opposition, only to be confronted by the prosaic compromises and realities of government, another form of coarse political language comes into its own – cries of hypocrisy, betrayal and moral turpitude. I was, alas, not the first nor the last politician who was unable to do in government all that I had said in opposition. Politicians claiming more than they are able actually to do in reality is not new and, I suspect, will be with us for a long time.

A lot has been said about the coarsening of language through the development of social or information 'bubbles' fostered, it is suggested, by social media. But these bubbles are not new either. The social identities we all construct, the accents that we have or affect, the clothes we wear, the schools we choose to send our children to, the cars we buy, the homes we live in, the holidays we go on, the friends we keep, the newspapers we read; all of these things make up the social 'bubbles' in which each of us operates. Britain is still a stubbornly class-ossified society and these subtle, or not so subtle, accoutrements of class identity enveloped Britons in their everyday lives long before social media existed.

So insults, unparliamentary language, the coarse use of vitriol in public and political life, the volatility of elevated expectations and crashing disappointments about our politicians and the bubbles that we all create for ourselves individually and collectively are – none of them – new.

And yet, something seems to be afoot that is qualitatively new. First, technology is allowing us to tailor our consumption of news and culture around our own personal tastes. The days – no doubt romanticised with hindsight – when different generations would sit on the family sofa watching a limited, but shared, number of options on terrestrial television together are giving way to living rooms where everyone is on their own phone, tablet or laptop consuming a dizzying array of personalised content. Younger consumers, in particular, are turning away from shared, public outlets in favour of their own, personalised services.

Recently, I was having my hair cut. The young woman who was cutting my hair had a spectacular tattoo of an octopus on each arm, and when I asked her why she had them, she said she loved octopuses; she thought they were the most beautiful creatures on Earth. So I said she must enjoy David Attenborough's *Blue Planet II*, which had been compulsive viewing on the BBC for me and my family at the time. She said, 'I can't watch it.' When I asked her why not, she told me that she didn't have a TV licence: she didn't see the point. 'So what do you watch?' I asked her. 'I just love bingeing on Netflix boxsets,' she said.

Her attitude would send a chill down the spines of the BBC's executive team. Eighty-two percent of viewers aged 16–24 watch more than one episode of their favourite television series in a row each month. More than one in ten in this age group say they binge-watch every day. Over 64s watched an average of 5 hours and 44 minutes of terrestrial, old-fashioned broadcast TV per day in 2016, up by 50 minutes compared to 2006. By contrast, the amount of terrestrial TV watched daily by 16–24-year-olds has declined by 41 minutes since 2006. There are seven seasons, that's 115 hours, of *The West Wing*. Eight seasons, 138 hours, of *24*. Two hundred and thirty-seven episodes of *The Big Bang Theory* and 208 episodes of *How I Met Your Mother*. I myself am furiously catching up on *Breaking Bad*, a superb series that was in its heyday when I was in government and I didn't watch much television at all.

Your viewing and listening habits, just like my hairdresser's and the habits of many millions of our fellow citizens, particularly youngsters, are changing radically. Since technology allows us to tailor the content we consume – drama, music, culture, debate, news – to suit our own tastes, why wouldn't we exploit those opportunities to the full? Much has been written and said about society's use of Twitter or its attachment to Facebook's newsfeed, but the truth is that this pattern – of personalised consumption of news and culture – goes far wider. I love listening to music. I listen to music every day provided to me by Spotify, which offers me endless prompts on the music I might want to explore based on an algorithmic diagnosis of the music I have already listened to. The growing popularity of podcasts is another sign of the same trend: people want to immerse themselves in the content they enjoy at a pace and a time that suits them. Technology has helped us to inhabit our tastes more deeply and richly, and we are more enveloped in our tastes and opinions than ever before.

The relevance of this trend for political rhetoric and debate is complex. Some commentators breezily condemn the personalised consumption of information online, especially on social media, as the source for extreme and polarised political opinions. It is certainly true to say that one of the defining features of the internet is the ability it grants us to seek out and find others who share our interests and perspective beyond the bounds of our geographical communities. Yet there is little hard evidence that political polarisation coincided with the advent of social media (in the US, for example, academic studies have shown that political polarisation accelerated sharply in the 1990s, then grew only moderately, before accelerating again in recent years[44]). There is also evidence that the range of friends people generally have on social media means that the news posts to which they are exposed are in fact more diverse than the partisan coverage in much of the traditional mainstream media.[45]

Others have pointed to the raucous, unmediated nature of online debate (witness the online comments section of any major UK newspaper) and have blamed it for the coarsening of our politics. Again, there is something inherently liberating about the ability to express our thoughts freely online, and it's not surprising that the result isn't always an orderly and respectful debate grounded in evidence. That is the democratising effect of the internet: it provides a voice to millions of citizens who were previously excluded from the mainstream debate, and it provides an unprecedented ability to hold the powerful to account. As a democrat, I believe that is an overwhelmingly good thing, although of course it creates new and unpredictable effects. The jury is still out on the relative impact of these new forms of self-expression on voting behaviour but, in the parts of the world where 'elite opinion' has long held sway, there is no doubt that it has changed the political terms of trade.

Either way, the combination of unprecedented free expression and the personalisation of consumption – a trend as prevalent in the offline world as the online world (from fast fashion to YouTube recommendation algorithms) – may mean that we are, in general, less disposed to compromise in politics. If we can increasingly tailor the world to suit our own needs in our everyday lives as consumers, perhaps it is becoming a little harder to accept that we cannot get everything we want in politics as voters?

Second, political reporting. Just as its readership has declined, the traditional print media's partisanship, certainly on atom-splitting issues such as Brexit, has mutated into semi-permanent vitriol. There are many reasons for this. Large parts of our print media, more than ever before, are now owned or edited by a remarkably small clique of older men with particular views on some of the key issues of the day. They express their views through the newspapers under their control. They include the Barclay brothers, Rupert Murdoch and Paul Dacre, the immensely powerful former editor of the *Daily Mail*. It is remarkable how the frame of reference and debate set by significant, bestselling parts of the newspaper industry have been shaped by a small and ideologically homogenous cabal of older men who are neither accountable to, nor representative of, wider society. That seems to me both to be dangerous for the quality of our democracy and to have contributed to a semi-hysterical tone on many sensitive issues.

This was on ample display at the time of the EU referendum. The *Daily Mail,* for instance, whipped itself up into a frenzy, particularly around the issue of immigration. It is said that, in the lead-up to the referendum, there was a conversation between Paul Dacre and David Cameron in the Prime Minister's flat. Presumably Cameron called the meeting in order to try to persuade Dacre to take a more rounded view of what was at stake. It is said that Dacre pointed to a television in the corner of the room on which the evening news was showing. At that time, the daily news was dominated by the Mediterranean migration crisis. Referring to the pictures of those desperate people fleeing to south-eastern Europe to escape the violence and conflict in Syria, Dacre apparently said, 'Prime Minister, that is the reason you're going to lose the referendum.'

So it seems that Dacre realised, cynically but with great prescience, that if he and others were able to conflate in the public imagination our membership of the EU with the Mediterranean migration crisis and its mismanagement by EU member states at the time, many people would recoil from continued membership. We all remember the chaotic scenes of barbed wire being mounted at borders in south-eastern Europe, refugee camps in abysmal conditions being established in a rush and the terrorist incidents in Brussels and Paris at the time.

Dacre seemingly realised, more clearly than anyone else involved in the campaign, that if these things – terrorism, the Mediterranean migration crisis and our membership of the EU – could be linked, people would, entirely logically, vote to leave. On 17 out of the 23 weekdays before the referendum, the *Daily Mail* led with the immigration narrative, usually accompanied with lurid photographs and headlines such as 'EU killers and rapists we've failed to deport',[46] 'Cameron's migration deception'[47] and even a story about a one-legged Albanian double killer.[48] That hyperbole was only outdone after the referendum when the *Daily Mail* felt that its victory might slip from its grasp. You will all recall splenetic headlines such as 'Enemies of the People'[49] and 'Crush the Saboteurs',[50] aimed at those who did not drink the Brexit Kool-Aid in the way that clearly was deemed compulsory.

This isn't a point about how popular the newspapers are: only 3% of the British population actually reads the *Daily Mail*, for example. Nor do people read a paper and say to themselves,

'I'll follow the instruction of the editor on how I should vote or think'. Of course people have a much more sophisticated relationship with the papers they read and the information they consume. My point is about the way in which the newspapers are conducting their political reporting on issues on which they have ideologically strong views and the effect it has on the quality and tone of wider political debate.

I was active in politics on and off for 20 years or more, as an MP and as an MEP before that, and I cannot remember another occasion where so-called mainstream newspapers mutated so sharply from news organisations into aggressive, campaigning organisations. In doing so, they elevated themselves above other pillars in our democratic system: condemning judges simply for doing their job in an independent judiciary or the Governor of the Bank of England simply for giving his disinterested advice. A healthy democracy – including healthy political debate – depends on checks and balances in society. It is ironic that some of the traditional guardians of free speech have been the first to intimidate the freedom of expression of others.

Third, voting habits. There is a new volatility in the way in which people choose the parties they wish to vote for. This has been growing for a long time. The days when people voted for the same party as their mothers and fathers, their grandfathers and grandmothers, the other people on their street and in their communities: those days are long gone. In many ways, that is a very good thing. It marks an end to diffidence, to the hand-me-down generational attitude towards voting. As described earlier, we are all, as consumers, empowered in a way that is unparalleled in human history. We all face a dizzying array of choice – much of it available at the click of a mouse. That more autonomous, empowered attitude towards life has been replicated in politics, so people are now much more ready than they were in the past to think they'll try a splash of red in one election, and then, not liking that much, try a splash of blue in the next or even a dash of yellow in between. There is a jumpy volatility to politics that is reflected across the developed world. This is, broadly, a very good thing because it makes sure that those who are elected, who are there to serve the public, are less able and less inclined to take voters for granted. Voters will take away what they have given much more rapidly than has been the case in the past.

But this volatility lends itself to rapid 'mood swings' in politics. I experienced it fleetingly in 2010 when I was elevated (in a moment dubbed 'Cleggmania') to a gravity-defying pedestal, as if I were capable of remarkable feats of political wizardry, before – obviously – crashing down to earth with a bump. Jeremy Corbyn has been held aloft in this curious personality cult of 'Corbynmania' that sustains some of his core supporters, in which the expectations of what he is able to deliver, if he were ever to become prime minister, have run far in excess of what he would be able to do in government.

All politicians, including prime ministers and cabinets of all descriptions, are much less powerful than they're held to be. The globalised economy means that some of the big things asked of governments are entirely beyond the control of national politicians. And yet, like mice running in a wheel, they – and we, the electorate – feel we have to continually perpetuate the myth that somehow everything is in the gift of politicians.

We might reasonably ask why politicians can't be more candid about the limits to their powers. But just imagine if a politician knocked on your door at election time and said, 'Actually I'm not as powerful as you think, and I really can't fix everything though I will try terribly hard'. Their rival promising the moon on a stick would win hands down. I'd love to think that, at campaign time, we could paint in pastel colours and introduce all the nuances and subtleties of policymaking, but we can't and we're all complicit in that. Maybe the politicians should be a little bit more forthright about the restraints and realities of governing in a complex world. But maybe also we – and I now speak as an ex-politician and a voter – need to be a little bit more permissive of the reality of government, especially as we are assailed by global economic challenges, climate change, cross-border crime, terrorism, cybersecurity and more. These are all issues in which the nation state can play an important role but can never provide the full solution.

One of the reasons we have a crisis of legitimacy in our democracy is that, to almost all of those problems, you need to apply a supranational, international response. In other words, you need to beef up the capacity of governments to act together and yet, for all sorts of complex reasons, we are retreating from that very principle. Just as true globalism is needed more than ever before to tackle truly global problems, the politics of protectionism, nativism and nationalism are on the rise. Populism is on the rise too. Populism isn't always bad: Mahatma Gandhi was a populist of sorts. Populism, as a legitimate cry of anger against a deficient status quo or an unfeeling elite, is a powerful antidote to complacency, corruption and nepotism in politics. But the problem with most populists is that they trade in false hope: 'Build a wall and all will be well!' 'Quit Europe and the future will be bright!' 'Keep the immigrants out and your children will thrive!' Populism is often vindictive because it seeks to attack something or some people who are held to be responsible for wider ills. It falsely suggests that complex problems can all be reduced to simple solutions.

But where does the rage go when populism doesn't work? What will happen in those many deprived communities in the UK where people voted for Brexit in their droves when the Brexit land of milk and honey does not materialise? I'd love to think that everyone will become ardent Liberal Democrat-voting pro-Europeans. But I somehow doubt it. The likelihood, instead, is that voters will turn to the next populist who will come along with ever more extreme solutions to the continued injustices that they are enduring. In other words, my worry is that the anger and simplicities of populist politics do not collapse under the weight of their own contradictions but generate a ratchet effect towards greater political polarisation instead. And when the populists fail to deliver their utopia, they will have to find someone to blame. So be braced, be ready. Mountains of blame will be heaped upon the French, the Germans, Eurocrats and civil servants in the months and years ahead as the Brexit dream turns into a rancid narrative of betrayal instead.

Just at the very moment our country should be embarking on a profound process of social and economic renewal – from house building to apprenticeships, from mental health provision to pay progression – we find ourselves immersed instead in the quicksands of internal division and dwindling international relevance brought about in the wake of the Brexit referendum.

Some of these things will pass, eventually: new newspaper editors and proprietors will come along; brave and inspiring politicians will emerge; young people will demand to have another say on Europe; technology will continue to evolve.

But the elixir, the lifeblood, of a mature democracy, above and beyond its essential institutional components, is the ability to bridge and accommodate differences in a plural society in which there are competing claims on public resources and competing ideologies and interests. In a mature democracy, we all agree to engage in a spirit of give and take: sometimes this lot wins, the next time the other lot wins, and so on. We accommodate our differences: that's the genius of democracy. It is not a 'winner permanently takes all' system. Competing interests constantly jostle and no single interest, no single section of society, no single collection of opinions is utterly disenfranchised or completely victorious. Everybody feels they have their place in that raucous debate that makes up our democracy.

My worry about the vituperation colouring so much of our political debate is that it makes the idea of give and take increasingly unworkable. The idea that those with whom you disagree have just as much of a right to their opinions or their dreams or aspirations as you do, and that the losing side in an election, or in a referendum, has a vital role in democratic debate, is a precious one that is under sustained attack.

It's one of the reasons why I believe it was such a fatal error, in the wake of the narrowly determined Brexit referendum, for the victors to ignore the wishes of the losing side (close to half the voting public), and instead to declare that those who voted to remain (including over 70% of young voters) in effect no longer had any legitimate voice in shaping what would come next. I think that is fundamentally incompatible with how a mature democracy should operate. In a democracy, you should never leave the losing side entirely empty handed.

Whether it is vitriol in political speech or hyper-personalised consumerism, whether it's the ferocious partisanship of some newspapers or the rise of voting volatility and populism, all of these things combine to create something that is very dangerous to the fabric of our democracy: an intolerance of those who are in a minority, an intolerance of those who have lost and an intolerance of those who hold views that are not fashionable. That is something we must resist at all costs.

Notes

1   Parliament must not pass laws that infringe the European Convention on Human Rights, but it can and does argue with them, for example over enfranchising prisoners, and it can choose to take Britain out of membership of the Council of Europe (not the EU) which binds it to the Convention. See Claire Foster-Gilbert (ed.) *The Power of Judges* (London, Haus Publishing, 2018) pp. 7–8.

2   YouGov survey for *The Sunday Times* published 16 June 2019.

3   Jonathan Sumption, 'Shifting the Foundations', 5th Reith Lecture (BBC, 18 June 2019).

4   Chris Bryant, *Parliament, The Biography, Volume I: Ancestral Voices* and *Volume II: Reform* (London, Transworld Publishers, 2014).

5   David Natzler, Preface, *Erskine May: Parliamentary Practice* (London, LexisNexis, 2019).

6   Declared, among many other places, in his dialogue in Claire Foster-Gilbert (ed.), *The Power of Civil Servants* (London, Haus Publishing, 2018) p. 35.

7   Igor Judge, 'Constitutional Change: Unfinished Business', in *The Safest Shield: Lectures, Speeches and Essays* (Oxford, Hart Publishing, 2015) p. 75.

8   Lord Sumption, 'Supreme Court ruling is the natural result of Boris Johnson's constitutional vandalism', *The Times*, 24 September 2019.

9   Committee on Standards in Public Life, *Intimidation in Public Life: A Review by the Committee on Standards in Public Life* (London, CSPL, 2018). A Hansard search revealed 19 references to death threats made to MPs in the last five years. C.f. also, e.g., '"Abuse is virtually constant": female MPs speak about the threats they face', *The Guardian*, 26 September 2019.

10   The Constitutional Reform and Governance Act 2010 put the Civil Service Code into law. See the discussion of this in Claire Foster-Gilbert (ed.) *The Power of Civil Servants* (London, Haus Publishing, 2018).

11   'Special advisers' are not civil servants but work directly for ministers and are appointed by them. Their explicitly political role is circumscribed.

12   Clare Moriarty, 'Values and Values Conflict in the Civil Service' (London, Department for Transport, 2006).

13   The Civil Service Code. Quoted in Claire Foster-Gilbert, op. cit. p. 54.

14   Ibid. p. 58.

15   Thomas Nagel, *The View from Nowhere* (Oxford, Oxford University Press, 1989).

16   A personal opinion expressed by a senior civil servant during a private conversation with Claire Foster-Gilbert.

17   For our detailed discussion of the reality and importance of truth, see Claire Foster-Gilbert (ed.)

Truth in Public Life (London, Haus Publishing, in press).

18   Headline, *Daily Mail*, 4 November 2016.

19   R (on the application of Miller and another) (Respondents) v Secretary of State for Exiting the European Union (Appellant), 24 January 2017.

20   R (on the application of Miller) (Appellant) v The Prime Minister (Respondent); Cherry and others (Respondents) v Advocate General for Scotland (Appellant) (Scotland), 24 September 2019.

21   Boris Johnson, Prime Minister's Update (London, Hansard, 25 September 2019) column 775.

22   Such a view takes the Treasury, on the north side of Parliament Square, to represent the Executive.

23   C.f. my essays in Claire Foster-Gilbert (ed.) *Integrity in Public Life* (London, Haus Publishing, 2019) and *Truth in Public Life* (London, Haus publishing, in press).

24   Speech delivered in the Guildhall (London, 9 November 1866).

25   Cited in Eli Zaretsky, 'Trump's Charisma', *London Review of Books*, 27 June 2019.

26   By means, *inter alia*, of its Fellows' Programme and seminars for parliamentarians and government departments.

27   Jean Vanier (1928–2019) founded the L'Arche movement of communities in which the able-bodied both served and learned from the disabled.

28   Angus Ritchie, 'Populism and the Politics of Jesus', togetherforthecommongood.co.uk, accessed 19 September 2019.

29 Winston Churchill, speech in a debate on the Parliament Bill (London, Hansard, 11 November 1947) paragraph 207.

30 Costica Bradatan, 'Democracy Is for the Gods', *New York Times*, 5 July 2019.

31 Harper Lee, *To Kill a Mockingbird* (London, Arrow Books, 1960) p. 33.

32 See 'Executive Summary', The SDG16 Data Initiative 2017 Global Report, web.archive.org/web/20181020133024/http:/www.sdg16report.org/, accessed 15 October 2019.

33 The phrase 'one of us' is associated with Margaret Thatcher, who initially used the term to refer to reliable colleagues. See Hugo Young, Preface, *One of Us* (London, Pan Books, 2013).

34 'Back to basics' was a phrase used by Sir John Major in 1993 with the intention of promoting traditional values. It became associated with socially conservative causes and was followed by accusations that Conservative Party politicians were not upholding the moral standards the phrase implied.

35 Anthony Trollope, *The Life of Cicero* (London, Forgotten Books, 2012) p. 82.

36 Edmund Burke, 'Speech at the Conclusion of the Poll at Bristol', in *Reflections on the Revolution in France and other writings* (London, Everyman's Library, 2015) p. 151.

37 Coined by Evelyn Beatrice Hall writing as S.G. Tallentyre, *The Friends of Voltaire* (London, John Murray, 1906) pp. 198, 199.

38 Winston Churchill, op. cit.

39 Harold Macmillan, Address to the Parliament of South Africa, 3 February 1960.

40 The Devlin Report was the result of an inquiry into the state of emergency declared in Nyasaland (a British Protectorate at the time and now part of Malawi) in 1959 in response to protests and growing unrest. The report was critical of the Nyasaland Government and referred to the Protectorate as a 'police state'.

41 The Scott Inquiry, commissioned in 1992, investigated the sale of arms to Iraq by British companies and the involvement of the Government. The resulting report included criticisms of government procedures and the actions of individual ministers.

42 Petronius, *Satyricon*, 58.

43 Plautus, *Mercator*, Act I, Scene II.

44 See Yochai Benkler, Robert Faris and Hal Roberts, *Network Propaganda: Manipulation, Disinformation and Radicalization in American Politics* (Oxford, Oxford University Press, 2018) p. 291.

45 See Richard Fletcher and Joy Jenkins, 'Polarisation and the News Media in Europe', Reuters Institute for the Study of Journalism, March 2019.

46 Headline, *Daily Mail*, 3 June 2016.

47 Headline, *Daily Mail*, 21 June 2016.

48 Story in the *Daily Mail*, 8 June 2016.

49 Headline, *Daily Mail*, 4 November 2016.

50 Headline, *Daily Mail*, 19 April 2017.

WESTMINSTER ABBEY INSTITUTE

The Responsibilities of Democracy is published in partnership with Westminster Abbey Institute. Westminster Abbey launched its Institute in 2013 to work with the people and institutions by whom it is surrounded in Parliament Square to revitalise moral and spiritual values in public life. It offers space and time for challenging conversation and quiet reflection to people of all faiths and none.

In doing so, the Institute aims to remind those who govern of their vocation to public service, helping them to grow in moral sensitivity and resilience and to better define the good they are trying to do.

HAUS CURIOSITIES

Inspired by the topical pamphlets of the interwar years, as well as by Einstein's advice to 'never lose a holy curiosity', the series presents short works of opinion and analysis by notable figures. Under the guidance of the series editor, Peter Hennessy, Haus Curiosities have been published since 2014.

Welcoming contributions from a diverse pool of authors, the series aims to reinstate the concise and incisive booklet as a powerful strand of politico-literary life, amplifying the voices of those who have something urgent to say about a topical theme.

'Nifty little essays – the thinking person's commuting read'
– *The Independent*

*Britain in a Perilous World: The Strategic
Defence and Security Review We Need*
by Jonathan Shaw

*The UK's In-Out Referendum: EU Foreign
and Defence Policy Reform*
by David Owen

Establishment and Meritocracy
by Peter Hennessy

Greed: From Gordon Gekko to David Hume
by Stewart Sutherland

*The Kingdom to Come: Thoughts on the Union
Before and After the Scottish Referendum*
by Peter Hennessy